PHILOSOPHY AND POLITICS

PHILOSOPHY AND POLITICS

·•ઝ··ઝ ૄ··ૄ··

BERTRAND RUSSELL F.R.S.

LONDON

PUBLISHED FOR THE

NATIONAL BOOK LEAGUE

BY THE CAMBRIDGE UNIVERSITY PRESS

1947

CAMBRIDGE
UNIVERSITY PRESS

University Printing House, Cambridge CB2 8BS, United Kingdom

Cambridge University Press is part of the University of Cambridge.

It furthers the University's mission by disseminating knowledge in the pursuit of
education, learning and research at the highest international levels of excellence.

www.cambridge.org
Information on this title: www.cambridge.org/9781316612927

© Cambridge University Press 1947

First published 1947
First paperback edition 2016

A catalogue record for this publication is available from the British Library

ISBN 978-1-316-61292-7 Paperback

PHILOSOPHY AND POLITICS

꙰꙰꙰꙰꙰꙰

THE British are distinguished among the nations of modern Europe, on the one hand by the excellence of their philosophers, and on the other hand by their contempt for philosophy. In both respects they show their wisdom. But contempt for philosophy, if developed to the point at which it becomes systematic, is itself a philosophy; it is the philosophy which, in America, is called "instrumentalism". I suggest that philosophy, if it is bad philosophy, may be dangerous, and therefore deserves that degree of negative respect which we accord to lightning and tigers. What positive respect may be due to "good" philosophy I will leave for the moment an open question.

The connection of philosophy with politics, which is the subject of my lecture, has been less evident in Britain than in Continental countries. Empiricism, broadly speaking, is connected with liberalism, but Hume was a Tory; what philosophers call "idealism" has, in general, a similar connection with conservatism, but T. H. Green was a Liberal. On the Continent distinctions have been more clear cut, and there has been a greater readiness to accept or reject a block of doctrines as a whole, without critical scrutiny of each separate part.

In most civilised countries at most times, philosophy has been a matter in which the authorities had an official opinion, and except where liberal democracy prevails this is still the case. The Catholic Church is committed to the philosophy of Aquinas, the Soviet Government to that of Marx. The Nazis upheld German idealism, though the degree of allegiance to be given to Kant, Fichte or Hegel

7

respectively was not clearly laid down. Catholics, Communists, and Nazis all consider that their views on practical politics are bound up with their views on theoretical philosophy. Democratic liberalism, in its early successes, was connected with the empirical philosophy developed by Locke. I want to consider this relation of philosophies to political systems as it has in fact existed, and to inquire how far it is a valid logical relation, and how far, even if not logical, it has a kind of psychological inevitability. In so far as either kind of relation exists, a man's philosophy may have an intimate connection with the happiness or misery of large sections of mankind.

The word "philosophy" is one of which the meaning is by no means fixed. Like the word "religion", it has one sense when used to describe certain features of historical cultures, and another when used to denote a study or an attitude of mind which is considered desirable in the present day. Philosophy, as pursued in the universities of the Western democratic world, is, at least in intention, part of the pursuit of knowledge, aiming at the same kind of detachment as is sought in science, and not required, by the authorities, to arrive at conclusions convenient to the government. Many teachers of philosophy would repudiate, not only the intention to influence their pupils' politics, but also the view that philosophy should inculcate virtue. This, they would say, has as little to do with the philosopher as with the physicist or the chemist. Knowledge, they would say, should be the sole purpose of university teaching; virtue should be left to parents, schoolmasters, and churches.

But this view of philosophy, with which I have much sympathy, is very modern, and even in the modern world exceptional. There is a quite different view, which has prevailed since antiquity, and to which philosophy has owed its social and political importance.

Philosophy, in this historically usual sense, has resulted from the attempt to produce a synthesis of science and religion, or, perhaps more exactly, to combine a doctrine as to the nature of the universe and man's place in it with a practical ethic inculcating what was considered the best way of life. Philosophy was distinguished from religion by the fact that, nominally at least, it did not appeal to authority or tradition; it was distinguished from science by the fact that an essential part of its purpose was to tell men how to live. Its cosmological and ethical theories were closely interconnected: sometimes ethical motives influenced the philosopher's views as to the nature of the universe, sometimes his views as to the universe led him to ethical conclusions. And with most philosophers ethical opinions involved political consequences: some valued democracy, others oligarchy; some praised liberty, others discipline. Almost all types of philosophy were invented by the Greeks, and the controversies of our own day were already vigorous among the pre-Socratics.

The fundamental problem of ethics and politics is that of finding some way of reconciling the needs of social life with the urgency of individual desires. This has been achieved, in so far as it has been achieved, by means of various devices. Where a government exists, the criminal law can be used to prevent anti-social action on the part of those who do not belong to the government, and law can be reinforced by religion wherever religion teaches that disobedience is impiety. Where there is a priesthood sufficiently influential to enforce its moral code on lay rulers, even the rulers become to some extent subject to law; of this there are abundant instances in the Old Testament and in medieval history. Kings who genuinely believe in the Divine government of the world, and in a system of rewards and punishments in the next life, feel themselves not omnipotent, and not able to sin with

　　　　　　　　　　　　　　B

impunity. This feeling is expressed by the King in *Hamlet*, when he contrasts the inflexibility of Divine justice with the subservience of earthly judges to the royal power.

Philosophers, when they have tackled the problem of preserving social coherence, have sought solutions less obviously dependent upon dogma than those offered by official religions. Most philosophy has been a reaction against scepticism; it has arisen in ages when authority no longer sufficed to produce the socially necessary minimum of belief, so that nominally rational arguments had to be invented to secure the same result. This motive has led to a deep insincerity infecting most philosophy, both ancient and modern. There has been a fear, often unconscious, that clear thinking would lead to anarchy, and this fear has led philosophers to hide in mists of fallacy and obscurity.

There have, of course, been exceptions; the most notable are Protagoras in antiquity, and Hume in modern times. Both, as a result of scepticism, were politically conservative. Protagoras did not know whether the gods exist, but he held that in any case they ought to be worshipped. Philosophy, according to him, had nothing edifying to teach, and for the survival of morals we must rely upon the thoughtlessness of the majority and their willingness to believe what they had been taught. Nothing, therefore, must be done to weaken the popular force of tradition.

The same sort of thing, up to a point, may be said about Hume. After setting forth his sceptical conclusions, which, he admits, are not such as men can live by, he passed on to a piece of practical advice which, if followed, would prevent anybody from reading him. "Carelessness and inattention", he says, "alone can afford us any remedy. For this reason I rely entirely upon them". He does not, in this connection, set forth his reasons for being a Tory, but it is obvious that "carelessness and inattention", while they may lead to acquiescence in the *status quo*, can-

10

not, unaided, lead a man to advocate this or that scheme of reform.

Hobbes, though less sceptical than Hume, was equally persuaded that government is not of divine origin, and was equally led, by the road of disbelief, to advocacy of extreme conservatism.

Protagoras was "answered" by Plato, and Hume by Kant and Hegel. In each case the philosophical world heaved a sigh of relief, and refrained from examining too nicely the intellectual validity of the "answer", which in each case had political as well as theoretical consequences —though in the case of the "answer" to Hume, it was not the Liberal Kant but the reactionary Hegel who developed the *political* consequences.

But thorough-going sceptics, such as Protagoras and Hume, have never been influential, and have served chiefly as bugbears to be used by reactionaries in frightening people into irrational dogmatism. The really powerful adversaries against whom Plato and Hegel had to contend were not sceptics, but empiricists, Democritus in the one case and Locke in the other. In each, empiricism was associated with democracy and with a more or less utilitarian ethic. In each case, the new philosophy succeeded in presenting itself as nobler and more profound than the philosophy of pedestrian common sense which it superseded. In each case, in the name of all that was most sublime, the new philosophy made itself the champion of injustice, cruelty, and opposition to progress. In the case of Hegel this has come to be more or less recognised; in the case of Plato it is still something of a paradox, though it has been brilliantly advocated in a recent book by Dr. K. R. Popper.*

Plato, according to Diogenes Laertius, expressed the

* *The Open Society and its Enemies*. The same thesis is maintained in my *History of Western Philosophy*.

11

view that all the books of Democritus ought to be burnt. His wish was so far fulfilled that none of the writings of Democritus survive. Plato, in his *Dialogues*, never mentioned him. Aristotle gave some account of his doctrines; Epicurus vulgarised him; and finally Lucretius put the doctrine of Epicurus into verse. Lucretius just survived, by a happy accident. To reconstruct Democritus from the controversy of Aristotle and the poetry of Lucretius is not easy; it is almost as if we had to reconstruct Plato from Locke's refutation of innate ideas and Vaughan's "I saw eternity the other night". Nevertheless enough can be done to explain and condemn Plato's hatred.

Democritus is chiefly famous as (along with Leucippus) the founder of atomism, which he advocated in spite of the objections of metaphysicians—objections which were repeated by their successors down to and including Descartes and Leibniz. His atomism, however, was only part of his general philosophy. He was a materialist, a determinist, a free thinker, a utilitarian who disliked all strong passions, a believer in evolution, both astronomical and biological.

Like the men of similar opinions in the eighteenth century, Democritus was an ardent democrat. "Poverty in a democracy", he says, "is as much to be preferred to what is called prosperity under despots as freedom is to slavery". He was a contemporary of Socrates and Protagoras, and a fellow townsman of the latter; he flourished during the early years of the Peloponnesian war, but may have died before it ended. That war concentrated the struggle that was taking place throughout the Hellenic world between democracy and oligarchy. Sparta stood for oligarchy; so did Plato's family and friends, who were thus led to become Quislings. Their treachery is held to have contributed to the defeat of Athens. After that defeat, Plato set to work to sing the praises of the victors by constructing a Utopia of which the main features were suggested by the constitution of Sparta. Such, however, was his artistic skill that Liberals never noticed his reactionary tendencies until his disciples Lenin and Hitler had supplied them with a practical exegesis.*

That Plato's *Republic* should have been admired, on its political side, by decent people, is perhaps the most astonishing example of literary snobbery in all history. Let us consider a few points in this totalitarian tract. The main purpose of education, to which everything else is subordinated, is to produce courage in battle. To this end, there is to be a rigid censorship of the stories told by mothers and nurses to young children; there is to be no reading of Homer because that degraded versifier makes heroes lament and gods laugh; the drama is to be forbidden because it contains villains and women; music is to be only of certain kinds, which, in modern terms, would be "Rule Britannia" and "The British Grenadiers". The government is to be in the hands of a small oligarchy, who are to practise trickery and lying—trickery in manipulating the drawing of lots for eugenic purposes, and elaborate lying to persuade the population that there are biological differences between the upper and lower classes. Finally, there is to be large-scale infanticide when children are born otherwise than as a result of governmental swindling.

Whether people are happy in this community does not matter, we are told, for excellence resides in the whole, not in the parts. Plato's City is a copy of the eternal City laid up in heaven; perhaps in heaven we shall enjoy the kind of existence it offers us, but if we do not enjoy it here on earth, so much the worse for us.

This system derives its persuasive force from the mar-

* In 1920 I compared the Soviet State to Plato's *Republic*, to the equal indignation of Communists and Platonists.

riage of aristocratic prejudice and "divine philosophy"; without the latter, its repulsiveness would be obvious. The fine talk about the good and the unchanging makes it possible to lull the reader into acquiescence in the doctrine that the good shall rule, and that their purpose should be to preserve the *status quo*, as the ideal State in heaven does. To every man of strong political convictions—and the Greeks had amazingly vehement political passions—it is obvious that "the good" are those of his own party, and that, if they could establish the Constitution they desire, no further change would be necessary. So Plato taught, but by concealing his thought in metaphysical mists he gave it an impersonal and disinterested appearance which deceived the world for ages.

The ideal of static perfection, which Plato derived from Parmenides and embodied in his theory of ideas, is one which is now generally recognised as inapplicable to human affairs. Man is a restless animal, not content, like the boa constrictor, to have a good meal once a month and sleep the rest of the time. Man needs, for his happiness, not only the enjoyment of this or that, but hope and enterprise and change. As Hobbes says, "felicity consisteth in prospering, not in having prospered". Among modern philosophers, the ideal of unending and unchanging bliss has been replaced by that of evolution, in which there is supposed to be an ordered progress towards a goal which is never quite attained, or at any rate has not been attained at the time of writing. This change of outlook is part of the substitution of dynamics for statics which began with Galileo, and which has increasingly affected all modern thinking, whether scientific or political.

Change is one thing, progress is another. "Change" is scientific, "progress" is ethical; change is indubitable, whereas progress is a matter of controversy. Let us first consider change, as it appears in science.

Until the time of Galileo, astronomers, following Aristotle, believed that everything in the heavens, from the moon upwards, is unchanging and incorruptible. Since Laplace, no reputable astronomer has held this view. Nebulæ, stars, and planets, we now believe, have all developed gradually. Some stars, for instance the companion of Sirius, are "dead". They have at some time undergone a cataclysm which has enormously diminished the amount of light and heat radiating from them. Our own planet, in which philosophers are apt to take an excessive parochial interest, was once too hot to support life, and will in time be too cold. After ages during which the earth produced harmless trilobites and butterflies, evolution progressed to the point at which it generated Neros, Jenghiz Khans, and Hitlers. This, however, is a passing nightmare; in time the earth will become again incapable of supporting life, and peace will return.

But this purposeless see-saw, which is all that science has to offer, has not satisfied the philosophers. They have professed to discover a formula of progress, showing that the world was becoming gradually more and more to their liking. The recipe for a philosophy of this type is simple. The philosopher first decides which are the features of the existing world that give him pleasure, and which are the features that give him pain. He then, by a careful selection among facts, persuades himself that the universe is subject to a general law leading to an increase of what he finds pleasant and a decrease of what he finds unpleasant. Next, having formulated his law of progress, he turns on the public and says "It is fated that the world must develop as I say; therefore those who wish to be on the winning side, and do not care to wage a fruitless war against the inevitable, will join my party". Those who oppose him are condemned as unphilosophic, unscientific, and out of date, while those who agree with him feel assured of victory, since the universe is on their side. At the same time the winning side, for reasons which remain somewhat obscure, is represented as the side of virtue.

The man who first fully developed this point of view was Hegel. Hegel's philosophy is so odd that one would not have expected him to be able to get sane men to accept it, but he did. He set it out with so much obscurity that people thought it must be profound. It can quite easily be expounded lucidly in words of one syllable, but then its absurdity becomes obvious. What follows is not a caricature, though of course Hegelians will maintain that it is.

Hegel's philosophy, in outline, is as follows. Real Reality is timeless, as in Parmenides and Plato, but there is also an apparent reality, consisting of the everyday world in space and time. The character of real Reality can be determined by logic alone, since there is only one sort of possible Reality that is not self-contradictory. This is called the "Absolute Idea." Of this he gives the following definition: *"The Absolute Idea.* The idea, as unity of the subjective and objective Idea, is the notion of the Idea—a notion whose object is the Idea as such, and for which the objective is Idea—an Object which embraces all characteristics in its unity". I hate to spoil the luminous clarity of this sentence by any commentary, but in fact, the same thing would be expressed by saying "The Absolute Idea is pure thought thinking about pure thought". Hegel has already proved to his satisfaction that all Reality is thought, from which it follows that thought cannot think about anything but thought, since there is nothing else to think about. Some people might find this a little dull; they might say: "I like thinking about Cape Horn and the South Pole and Mount Everest and the great nebula in Andromeda; I enjoy contemplating the ages when the earth was cooling while the sea boiled and volcanoes rose

16

and fell between night and morning. I find your precept, that I should fill my mind with the lucubrations of word-spinning professors, intolerably stuffy, and really, if that is your 'happy ending', I don't think it was worth while to wade through all the verbiage that led up to it". And with these words they would say goodbye to philosophy and live happy ever after.

But if we agreed with these people we should be doing Hegel an injustice, which God forbid. For Hegel would point out that, while the Absolute, like Aristotle's God, never thinks about anything but itself, because it knows that all else is illusion, yet we, who are forced to live in the world of phenomena, as slaves of the temporal process, seeing only the parts, and only dimly apprehending the whole in moments of mystic insight, we, illusory products of illusion, are compelled to think as though Cape Horn were self-subsistent and not merely an idea in the Divine Mind. When we think about Cape Horn, what happens in Reality is that the Absolute is aware of a Cape-Horny thought. It really does have such a thought, or rather such an aspect of the one thought that it timelessly thinks and is, and this is the only reality that belongs to Cape Horn. But since we cannot reach such heights, we are doing our best in thinking of it in the ordinary geographical way.

But what, some one may say, has all this to do with politics? At first sight, perhaps, not very much. To Hegel, however, the connection is obvious. It follows from his metaphysic that true liberty consists in obedience to an arbitrary authority, that free speech is an evil, that absolute monarchy is good, that the Prussian State was the best existing at the time when he wrote, that war is good, and that an international organisation for the peaceful settlement of disputes would be a misfortune.

It is just possible that some among my hearers may not see at once how these consequences follow, so I hope I may be pardoned for saying a few words about the intermediate steps.

Although time is unreal, the series of appearances which constitutes history has a curious relation to Reality. Hegel discovered the nature of Reality by a purely logical process called the "dialectic", which consists of discovering contradictions in abstract ideas and correcting them by making them less abstract. Each of these abstract ideas is conceived as a stage in the development of "The Idea", the last stage being the "Absolute Idea".

Oddly enough, for some reason which Hegel never divulged, the temporal process of history repeats the logical development of the dialectic. It might be thought, since the metaphysic professes to apply to all Reality, that the temporal process which parallels it would be cosmic, but not a bit of it: it is purely terrestial, confined to recorded history, and (incredible as this may seem) to the history that Hegel happened to know. Different nations, at different times, have embodied the stages of the Idea that the dialectic had reached at those times. Of China, Hegel knew only that it *was*, therefore China illustrated the category of mere Being. Of India he knew only that Buddhists believed in Nirvana, therefore India illustrated the category of Nothing. The Greeks and Romans got rather further along the list of categories, but all the late stages have been left to the Germans, who, since the time of the fall of Rome, have been the sole standard-bearers of The Idea, and had already in 1830 very nearly realized The Absolute Idea.

To any one who still cherishes the hope that man is a more or less rational animal, the success of this farrago of nonsense must be astonishing. In his own day, his system was accepted by almost all academically educated young Germans, which is perhaps explicable by the fact that it flattered German self-esteem. What is more surprising is its success outside Germany. When I was young, most teachers of philosophy in British and American universities were Hegelians, so that, until I read Hegel, I supposed there must be some truth in his system; I was cured, however, by discovering that everything he said on the philosophy of mathematics was plain nonsense.

Most curious of all was his effect on Marx, who took over some of his most fanciful tenets, more particularly the belief that history develops according to a logical plan, and is concerned, like the purely abstract dialectic, to find ways of avoiding self-contradiction. Over a large part of the earth's surface you will be liquidated if you question this dogma, and Western men of science who sympathize politically with Russia show their sympathy by using the word "contradiction" in ways that no self-respecting logician can approve.

In tracing a connection between the politics and the metaphysics of a man like Hegel, we must content ourselves with certain very general features of his practical programme. That Hegel glorified Prussia was something of an accident; in his earlier years he ardently admired Napoleon, and only became a German patriot when he became an employee of the Prussian State. Even in the latest form of his *Philosophy of History*, he still mentions Alexander, Caesar, and Napoleon as men great enough to have a right to consider themselves exempt from the obligations of the moral law. What his philosophy constrained him to admire was not Germany as against France, but order, system, regulation and intensity of governmental control. His deification of the State would have been just as shocking if the State concerned had been Napoleon's despotism. In his own opinion, he knew what the world needed, though most men did not; a strong government might compel men to act for the best, which democracy could never do. Heraclitus, to whom Hegel was

19

deeply indebted, says: "Every beast is driven to the pasture with blows". Let us, in any case, make sure of the blows; whether they lead to a pasture is a matter of minor importance—except, of course, to the "beasts".

It is obvious that an autocratic system, such as that advocated by Hegel or by Marx's present-day disciples, is only theoretically justifiable on a basis of unquestioned dogma. If you know for certain what is the purpose of the universe in relation to human life, what is going to happen, and what is good for people even if they do not think so; if you can say, as Hegel does, that his theory of history is "a result which happens to be known to *me*, because I have traversed the entire field"—then you will feel that no degree of coercion is too great, provided it leads to the goal.

The only philosophy that affords a theoretical justification of democracy in its temper of mind, is empiricism. Locke, who may be regarded, so far as the modern world is concerned, as the founder of empiricism, makes it clear how closely this is connected with his views on liberty and toleration and with his opposition to absolute monarchy. He is never tired of emphasizing the uncertainty of most of our knowledge, not with a sceptical intention such as Hume's, but with the intention of making men aware that they may be mistaken, and that they should take account of this possibility in all their dealings with men of opinions different from their own. He had seen the evils wrought both by the "enthusiasm" of the sectaries, and by the dogma of the divine right of kings; to both he opposed a piecemeal and patchwork political doctrine, to be tested at each point by its success in practice.

What may be called, in a broad sense, the Liberal theory of politics is a recurrent product of commerce. The first known example of it was in the Ionian cities of Asia Minor, which lived by trading with Egypt and Lydia.

When Athens, in the time of Pericles, became commercial, the Athenians became Liberal. After a long eclipse, Liberal ideas revived in the Lombard cities of the middle ages, and prevailed in Italy until they were extinguished by the Spaniards in the sixteenth century. But the Spaniards failed to reconquer Holland or to subdue England, and it was these countries that were the champions of Liberalism and the leaders in commerce in the seventeenth century. In our day the leadership has passed to the United States.

The reasons for the connection of commerce with Liberalism are obvious. Trade brings men into contact with tribal customs different from their own, and in so doing destroys the dogmatism of the untravelled. The relation of buyer and seller is one of negotiation between two parties who are both free; it is most profitable when the buyer or seller is able to understand the point of view of the other party. There is, of course, imperialistic commerce, where men are forced to buy at the point of the sword; but this is not the kind that generates Liberal philosophies, which have flourished best in trading cities that have wealth without much military strength. In the present day, the nearest analogue to the commercial cities of antiquity and the middle ages is to be found in small countries such as Switzerland, Holland, and Scandinavia.

The Liberal creed, in practice, is one of live-and-let-live, of toleration and freedom as far as public order permit, of moderation and absence of fanaticism in political programmes. Even democracy, when it becomes fanatical, as it did among Rousseau's disciples in the French Revolution, ceases to be Liberal; indeed, a fanatical belief in democracy makes democratic institutions impossible, as appeared in England under Cromwell and in France under Robespierre. The genuine Liberal does not say "this is true"; he says, "I am inclined to think that under present circumstances this opinion is probably the best" And it is only in this limited and undogmatic sense that he will advocate democracy.

What has theoretical philosophy to say that is relevant to the validity or otherwise of the Liberal outlook? The essence of the Liberal outlook lies not in *what* opinions are held, but in *how* they are held; instead of being held dogmatically, they are held tentatively, and with a consciousness that new evidence may at any moment lead to their abandonment. This is the way in which opinions are held in science, as opposed to the way in which they are held in theology. The decisions of the Council of Nicaea are still authoritative, but in science fourth-century opinions no longer carry any weight. In the U.S.S.R. the dicta of Marx on dialectical materialism are so unquestioned that they help to determine the views of geneticists on how to obtain the best breed of wheat,* though elsewhere it is thought that experiment is the right way to study such problems. Science is empirical, tentative and undogmatic; all immutable dogma is unscientific. The scientific outlook, accordingly, is the intellectual counterpart of what is, in the practical sphere, the outlook of Liberalism.

Locke, who first developed in detail the empiricist theory of knowledge, preached also religious toleration, representative institutions, and the limitation of governmental power by the system of checks and balances. Few of his doctrines were new, but he developed them in a weighty manner at just the moment when the English Government was prepared to accept them. Like the other men of 1688, he was only reluctantly a rebel, and he disliked anarchy as much as he disliked despotism. Both in intellectual and in practical matters he stood for order without authority; this might be taken as the motto both

* See *The New Genetics in the Soviet Union,* by Hudson and Richens, School of Agriculture, Cambridge, 1946.

of science and of Liberalism. It depends, clearly, upon consent or assent. In the intellectual world it involves standards of evidence which, after adequate discussion, will lead to a measure of agreement among experts. In the practical world it involves submission to the majority after all parties have had an opportunity to state their case.

In both respects his moment was a fortunate one. The great controversy between the Ptolemaic and the Copernican systems had been decided, and scientific questions could no longer be settled by an appeal to Aristotle. Newton's triumphs seemed to justify boundless scientific optimism. In the practical world, a century and half of wars of religion had produced hardly any change in the balance of power as between Protestants and Catholics. Enlightened men had begun to view theological controversies as an absurdity, caricatured in Swift's war between the Big-Endians and the Little-Endians. The extreme Protestant sects, by relying upon the inner light, had made what professed to be Revelation into an anarchic force. Delightful enterprises, scientific and commercial, invited energetic men to turn aside from barren disputation. Fortunately they accepted the invitation, and two centuries of unexampled progress resulted.

We are now again in an epoch of wars of religion, but a religion is now called an "ideology". At the moment the Liberal philosophy is felt by many to be too tame and middle-aged; the idealistic young look for something with more bite in it, something which has a definite answer to all their questions, which calls for missionary activity and gives hope of a millenium brought about by conquest. In short, we have been plunging into a renewed age of faith. Unfortunately the atomic bomb is a swifter exterminator than the stake, and cannot safely be allowed so long a run. We must hope that a more rational outlook can be made to prevail; for only through a revival of Liberal tentativeness and tolerance can our world survive.

The empiricist's theory of knowledge—to which, with some reservations, I adhere—is half way between dogma and scepticism. Almost all knowledge, it holds, is in some degree doubtful, though the doubt, if any, is negligible as regards pure mathematics and facts of present sense-perception. The doubtfulness of what passes for knowledge is a matter of degree; having recently read a book on the Anglo-Saxon invasion of Britain, I am now convinced of the existence of Hengist, but very doubtful about Horsa. Einstein's general theory of relativity is probably, broadly speaking, true, but when it comes to calculating the circumference of the universe we may be pardoned for expecting later investigations to give a somewhat different result. The modern theory of the atom has pragmatic truth, since it enables us to construct atomic bombs; its consequences are what instrumentalists facetiously call "satisfactory". But it is not improbable that some quite different theory may in time be found to give a better explanation of the observed facts. Scientific theories are accepted as useful hypotheses to suggest further research, and as having some element of truth in virtue of which they are able to colligate existing observations; but no sensible person regards them as immutably perfect.

In the sphere of practical politics, this intellectual attitude has important consequences. In the first place, it is not worth while to inflict a comparatively certain present evil for the sake of a comparatively doubtful future good. If the theology of former times was entirely correct, it was worth while burning a number of people at the stake in order that the survivors might go to heaven, but if it was doubtful whether heretics would go to hell, the argument for persecution was not valid. If it is certain that Marx's eschatology is true, and that as soon as private capitalism has been abolished we shall all be happy ever after, then it is right to pursue this end by means of dictatorships, concentration camps, and world wars; but if the end is doubtful or the means not sure to achieve it, present misery becomes an irresistible argument against such drastic methods. If it were certain that without Jews the world would be a paradise, there could be no valid objection to Auschwitz; but if it is much more probable that the world resulting from such methods would be a hell, we can allow free play to our natural humanitarian revulsion against cruelty.

Since, broadly speaking, the distant consequences of actions are more uncertain than the immediate consequences, it is seldom justifiable to embark on any policy on the ground that, though harmful in the present, it will be beneficial in the long run. This principle, like all others held by empiricists, must not be held absolutely; there are cases where the future consequences of one policy are fairly certain and very unpleasant, while the present consequences of the other, though not agreeable, are easily endurable. This applies, for instance, to saving food for the winter, investing capital in machinery, and so on. But even in such cases uncertainty should not be lost sight of. During a boom there is much investment that turns out to have been unprofitable, and modern economists recognize that the habit of investing rather than consuming may easily be carried too far.

It is commonly urged that, in a war between Liberals and fanatics, the fanatics are sure to win, owing to their more unshakeable belief in the righteousness of their cause. This belief dies hard, although all history, including that of the last few years, is against it. Fanatics have failed, over and over again, because they have attempted the impossible, or because, even when what they aimed at was possible, they were too unscientific to adopt the right

D

means; they have failed also because they roused the hostility of those whom they wished to coerce. In every important war since 1700 the more democratic side has been victorious. This is partly because democracy and empiricism (which are intimately interconnected) do not demand a distortion of facts in the interests of theory. Russia and Canada, which have somewhat similar climatic conditions, are both interested in obtaining better breeds of wheat; in Canada this aim is pursued experimentally, in Russia by interpreting the Marxist Scriptures.

Systems of dogma without empirical foundation, such as those of scholastic theology, Marxism, and fascism, have the advantage of producing a great degree of social coherence among their disciples. But they have the disadvantage of involving persecution of valuable sections of the population. Spain was ruined by the expulsion of the Jews and Moors; France suffered by the emigration of Huguenots after the Revocation of the Edict of Nantes; Germany would probably have been first in the field with the atomic bomb but for Hitler's hatred of Jews. And, to repeat, dogmatic systems have the two further disadvantages of involving false beliefs on practically important matters of fact, and of rousing violent hostility in those who do not share the fanaticism in question. For these various reasons, it is not to be expected that, in the long run, nations addicted to a dogmatic philosophy will have the advantage over those of a more empirical temper. Nor is it true that dogma is necessary for social coherence when social coherence is called for; no nation could have shown more of it than the British showed in 1940.

Empiricism, finally, is to be commended not only on the ground of its greater truth, but also on ethical grounds. Dogma demands authority, rather than intelligent thought, as the source of opinion; it requires persecution of heretics and hostility to unbelievers; its asks of its disciples that they should inhibit natural kindliness in favour of systematic hatred. Since argument is not recognized as a means of arriving at truth, adherents of rival dogmas have no method except war by means of which to reach a decision. And war, in our scientific age, means, sooner or later, universal death.

I conclude that, in our day as in the time of Locke, empiricist Liberalism (which is not incompatible with *democratic* socialism) is the only philosophy that can be adopted by a man who, on the one hand, demands some scientific evidence for his beliefs, and, on the other hand, desires human happiness more than the prevalence of this or that party or creed. Our confused and difficult world needs various things if it is to escape disaster, and among these one of the most necessary is that, in the nations which still uphold Liberal beliefs, these beliefs should be whole-hearted and profound, not apologetic towards dogmatisms of the right or the left, but deeply persuaded of the value of liberty, scientific freedom, and mutual forbearance. For without these beliefs life on our politically divided but technically unified planet will hardly continue to be possible.

READING LIST

PLATO (427–347 B.C.)

Translations:

JOWETT, BENJAMIN. *Republic.* (O.U.P.) 1908. 2 vols.
LINDSAY, A. D. *Republic.* (Dent) 1908.
HARWOOD, J. *The Platonic Epistles.* (O.U.P.) 1932.
TAYLOR, A. E. *The Laws.* (Dent) 1934.
LIVINGSTONE, RICHARD. *Selections from Plato.* (O.U.P.) 1940.
   Works. Greek Text with Translation. (Heinemann) 1919–1935.
   12 vols.

Criticism:

BURNET, J. *Greek Philosophy from Thales to Plato.* (O.U.P.) 1914.
CROSSMAN, R. H. *Plato Today.* (Allen & Unwin) 1937.
GROTE, GEORGE. *Plato and the Other Companions of Socrates.* London, 1867.
   3 vols.
TAYLOR, A. E. *Plato the Man and His Work.* (Methuen) 1926.

HOBBES, THOMAS (1588–1679)

   Leviathan. (Dent) 1914.
   Leviathan. (Blackwell, Oxford) 1946.

Criticism:

GOOCH, G. P. *Hobbes.* (O.U.P.) 1940.
STEPHEN, LESLIE. *Hobbes.* (Macmillan) 1904.

LOCKE, JOHN (1632–1704)

   An Essay concerning Human Understanding. (O.U.P.) 1894. 2 vols.
   The Second Treatise of Civil Government and *A Letter Concerning Toleration.*
   (Blackwell, Oxford) 1946.

HUME, DAVID (1711–1776)

   Treatise of Human Nature. (Dent) 1911.

Criticism:

KRUSE, L. *Hume's Philosophy in His Principal Work: a Treatise on Human
   Nature and in His Essays.* (O.U.P.) 1939.
SMITH, N. K. *Philosophy of David Hume.* (Macmillan) 1941.

KANT, IMMANUEL (1724–1804)

Translations:

MEIKLEJOHN, J. M. D. *Critique of Pure Reason.* (Dent) 1934.
MAHAFFY, J. P. *Prolegomena.* (Macmillan) 1915.
ABBOTT, T. K. *Critique of Practical Reason.* (Longmans) 1898.
BERNARD, J. H. *Critique of Judgment.* (Macmillan) 1914.

FICHTE, JOHANN GOTTLIEB (1762–1814)

Translations:
SMITH, WILLIAM. *Popular Writings of Fichte, with Memoir*. London, 1889. 2 vols.
JONES, R. S. and TURNBULL, G. H. *Addresses to the German Nation*. (Open Court) 1923.

HEGEL, GEORG WILHELM FRIEDRICH (1770–1831)

Translations:
DYDE, S. W. *Philosophy of Right*. (Bell) 1896.
SIBREE, J. *Philosophy of History*. (Bohn) 1857.
HALDANE, R. B. *A History of Philosophy*. (Kegan Paul) 1892–1896. 3 vols.

MILL, JOHN STUART (1806–1873)

On Liberty and *Considerations on Representative Government*. (Blackwell, Oxford) 1946.

MARX, KARL (1818–1883)

Translation:
MOORE, SAMUEL and AVELING, EDWARD. *Capital*. (Allen & Unwin) 1938.

LENIN, NIKOLAI (1870–1924)

Translation:
FINSBERG, A. *Materialism and Empirio-Criticism*. (Lawrence & Wishart) 1938.

GENERAL:

HOBHOUSE, L. T. *Metaphysical Theory of the State: a Criticism*. (Macmillan) 1918.
LASKI, H. J. *Political Thought in England: Locke to Bentham* (O.U.P.) 1920.
OAKESHOTT, M. *Social and Political Doctrines of Contemporary Europe*. (C.U.P.) 1939.
POPPER, K. R. *The Open Society and its Enemies*. (Routledge) 1945. 2 vols.
RUSSELL, BERTRAND. *The History of Western Philosophy*. (Allen & Unwin) 1946.
TAWNEY, R. H. *Religion and the Rise of Capitalism*. (Murray) 1926.